METROLINK
HANDBOOK
John A Senior and Colin Reeve

Not a scene in a Mediterranean city, but Manchester's Mosley Street in the summer of 2013 as a Metrolink tram from Bury heads for Droylsden via the East Manchester line. A perfect example of what can be achieved by pedestrianisation combined with an efficient light rail rapid transit system.

Transport in Manchester

The city of Manchester has always been at the forefront of passenger transport: John Greenwood's first British horse bus service in 1824, the Liverpool and Manchester Railway of 1830 with the world's first railway station, the Manchester Ship Canal of 1894 with its unique swinging aqueduct at Barton and the airfield at Hough End from where the world's first airline services commenced in 1919 all combined to place Manchester very firmly on the transport map. And now Manchester's Metrolink, incorporating on-street running, is the largest and most extensive of its kind in the United Kingdom.

From its earliest days Manchester's railway system suffered from a major problem: the city termini were located at the edge of the central area with no direct link between them or indeed into the city centre itself. Also, while the rapid growth of the railways quickly established its national and regional importance, the number of different companies building railways into Manchester with the amount of land required for stations and the lack of flexibility in a central area which was fast becoming built up, all combined to prevent the lines from penetrating further. Eventually, with rationalisation in the sixties, only two main termini remained, Piccadilly, originally opened in 1842 as London Road and serving routes to the south, and Victoria, dating from 1844 serving routes to the north.

The idea of linking the various railway stations first surfaced in 1839 when a plan was conceived for a tunnel under the city and in 1866 a lengthy viaduct was proposed. Around the turn of the century the idea was floated of a circular tunnel linking Victoria, London Road, Oxford Road, Central and Exchange stations in a similar fashion to the Glasgow subway. A similar plan was proposed in 1912, partly underground with eight city centre stations and a branch to serve the University, but this was abandoned two years later with the start of the First World War and it was never revived.

In the 1920s Manchester City Council formed an Underground Railway Special Committee and a system of some 14 miles was proposed in 1926 which would have covered the central area with extensions to Salford, Stretford and Prestwich. Two years later a more ambitious scheme of 35 miles was proposed comprising an inner and an outer circle linking the main stations with the city centre. It was estimated that the inner circle alone would carry 100 million passengers a year.

Henry Mattinson, Manchester's legendary Tramways General Manager, then produced a scheme combining underground and surface sections with a central interchange near the Town Hall, but this died with him in 1928. At this time the Manchester-Bury line, electrified since 1916, was the only electrified line in the city and the far-sighted Mattinson recommended more. The Altrincham line was electrified in 1931, but nothing more happened and the congested gap remained, to be bridged by various alternative tram and bus services for nearly forty years.

Across the city centre

In the meantime various plans were developed in an attempt to provide some form of inter-station transfers and city centre links, but it was not until the arrival of the motor bus that viable solutions became possible, the first service starting in the early thirties with a network of three routes linking the main stations and the city centre. These were eventually consolidated into one circular route which lasted until the outbreak of war in 1939.

After the war the last tram services were abandoned and some of the replacement buses passing London Road were extended to the forecourts of Victoria, Exchange and Central stations.

Then in 1961 a more ambitious scheme was introduced known as the City Circle, but this was doomed from the start as it fell foul of the powerful taxi lobby and was unable to access Piccadilly Station approach, thus being denied much of its intended traffic. After various cost-cutting measures it was withdrawn in 1965.

Once again passengers leaving their trains at Piccadilly or Victoria were left with the choice of a long walk or an expensive taxi ride to their eventual destinations. But then in 1974, with plans being developed for a heavy rail link, an interim solution was proposed for a high frequency midibus service linking the entrances to both stations through the central business and shopping districts of the city. Known as Centreline, and running every few minutes at a flat fare, this was implemented by the new Passenger Transport Executive despite the vociferous protests of the taxi owners and was the most successful of various schemes, lasting with only minor changes until the first stage of Metrolink rendered it redundant in 1995.

For over 140 years it had been necessary to change from rail to road at Piccadilly or Victoria stations before gaining access to the city centre. The high frequency Centreline service was the most successful of the various options tried, and lasted as an interim solution from 1974 until the opening of the first phase of Metrolink in 1992. A Centreline midibus is seen here loading outside the entrance to Piccadilly Station after the morning rush hour.

The concept of Metrolink

After 40 years of inactivity the next proposal came in 1966. This was for a suspended monorail to run between Middleton and Wythenshawe, linking with Manchester Airport and was followed by a proposal for a full-size (heavy) rapid transit line linking Ringway with Langley and then onward to Birch Services on the M62 motorway where a large park and ride area would be built. The intention was also to allow for later extensions to include British Rail routes to Bury, Oldham, Hyde, Romiley, Swinton, Eccles, Sale and Altrincham. This ambitious scheme foundered as its predecessors had, because of the cost.

The creation of the SELNEC Passenger Transport Authority and Executive in 1969 led to a proposal in their long-term plan, published in 1973, for a Piccadilly to Victoria tunnel to link suburban lines from Stockport and Wilmslow under the city to Bury and Bolton with intermediate stations under the Piccadilly Plaza and at the junction of Cross Street and Market Street. This got as far as Parliamentary approval and some trial digging, but once again government funding was not forthcoming and the scheme was abandoned by the newly-elected Greater Manchester Council in 1977. Meanwhile, the one mile gap between Manchester's two main railway stations remained, covered by the Centreline midibus service previously mentioned.

After the failure of the Picc-Vic tunnel proposal, a Rail Strategy Study was set up in 1982, the participants being the then Greater Manchester Council (abolished in 1986), Greater Manchester Passenger Transport Executive and British Rail. Their brief was to consider a wide range of options for the development of the rail network in the Greater Manchester region with particular emphasis on the long-standing problems of poor access to the city's central business area from the two major railway stations and the lack of a north-south route through the city centre.

Other problems which had developed over the years were the obsolescence of the rolling stock and signalling systems and the outworn as well as non-standard electrification systems on the Bury line (1200v dc 3rd rail) and the Hadfield/Glossop line (1500v dc overhead). The former Greater Manchester Council had advocated light rail systems in support of its plans for urban concentration, redirection to the inner core, maintenance of the regional centre and conservation of resources and amenities. Furthermore, British Rail and the PTE had already published proposals for the Windsor Link in Salford to enable trains from Bolton and the North West to reach Piccadilly station, and the Hazel Grove Chord to enable trains from Sheffield to run through Stockport to reach Piccadilly and on to Liverpool. These schemes would allow Intercity and Express services to be concentrated on Piccadilly. They were approved in due course, the Hazel Grove Chord opening in 1987 and the Windsor Link in 1988.

With regard to the PTE-supported local rail services, the Rail Strategy Study eventually decided upon the light rail option following engineering feasibility studies undertaken by consultant engineers, traffic management studies by the highway authority, and examination of the planning, economic and financial effects. Various forms of light rail and busways were investigated by visits to a number of European cities. Reserved busways

4

and guided busways were considered together with such extraneous options as monorails and automated guideway transit, but the outcome of the Study was that the technical and economic advantages of light rail would provide the most attractive and cost-effective solutions to Greater Manchester's protracted rail problems.

At an overall cost of £112 million for 20 route miles, ie £5.6 million per route mile, Metrolink was seen to be less costly than other comparable systems. The cost of the Tyne and Wear Metro was five times greater, and the cost of London's Docklands Light Rapid Transit system was costed at eight times greater per route mile.

With its combination of exclusive former British Rail lines, reserved street track and priority signalling, Metrolink was intended to improve access into the city centre, provide better links with the British Rail network, improve passengers' journeys both in time and quality, and reduce the level of revenue support for local rail services. In addition to combating the major historical problems associated with Manchester's rail communications, the long-term advantages were expected to include improvements to the environment including additional and extended pedestrian areas, a reduction in vehicular traffic in the city centre, overall financial and economic benefits for the area, encouragement for the development of vacant and derelict land, stimulation of leisure, recreation and tourist facilities, and the creation of new employment opportunities.

Another advantage of the Metrolink system was said to be the potential for extension. Further phases were anticipated which could be a combination of existing suburban railway lines and new lines. A line to Salford Quays on the site of the former docks, already a developing business, residential and leisure area, was seen as a priority and extensions to Oldham and Rochdale, Trafford Park and Didsbury were considered.

Metrolink was envisaged as complementing the network of British Rail services in Greater Manchester by providing a fully-integrated transport system incorporating the services of the many bus operators in the region. It was intended to demonstrate that public transport in the city and its environs can be attractive, convenient and efficient.

The extent to which this has been more than realised is a lasting tribute to the vision of the people who devised Metrolink and the drive and determination of those who pushed it through against all the odds, particularly the PTE's Chief Executive David Graham who tragically died in April 1991 shortly before his dream was fulfilled. Without his pragmatism and determination – "Either we do it this way or there will be no Metrolink" – it would have foundered like its predecessors.

Mr Graham, seen with Secretary of State for Transport Cecil Parkinson. Metrolink is a living memorial to David Graham's achievements.

From concept to tender

Following some six years of proposals, discussions, visits to other systems, negotiations with British Rail, meetings with the City Engineers and the Police, the local District Councils, and, not least, the Department of Transport, Greater Manchester PTE eventually obtained Government approval in January 1988 to go out to tender for the construction of the first phase of its Metrolink system.

What may not perhaps be appreciated is the enormous amount of preparatory work which was necessary: and its cost. The PTE estimated that it spent over £2m on this work, including consultancy fees, before it could seek tenders for the actual construction. The City Council also spent some £0.5m in planning, design approval and supervision to co-ordinate Metrolink into its traffic strategy, with a further £7m spent on moving the statutory services such as gas, electricity, water, sewage, telephone cables and the like which had been agreed should be moved away from the tracks to avoid future disruption of Metrolink services. This enormous burden, one which French systems, for example, do not have to bear, is now the subject of proposals that the utility companies themselves should foot the bill.

GMA, the successful consortium which constructed the system, estimated that its own costs to investigate and prepare design proposals and costings and submit these in the form of tenders came to hundreds of thousands of pounds, with similar costs to reach the second stage. Legal fees for preparation of contracts were also considerable.

So it will be appreciated that a very large amount of time and money needs to be spent in the tendering process long before any construction work can begin. All concerned believed that Government had seriously underestimated the magnitude and cost of this work, and indeed it admitted to being surprised that so few tenders were received. It must be understood that this is a system where "winner takes it all" as ABBA would put it, the unsuccessful bidders losing eye-watering sums of money with no recourse to compensation.

The detailed method of submitting tenders, examining and considering the documents and then receiving presentations from those who were seeking to gain the contract was extremely time-consuming. It was a vital part of the process and one which, with hindsight, needed even more time and resources than it was possible to make available in order to ensure that all parties' interests were fully considered and adequately covered by the Contract. Preparation of the legal documentation was also an extremely lengthy and very expensive business, the contracts forming a pile of paper well over two feet deep!

During the early years the PTE had expected that it would be responsible for the creation and operation of any light rail scheme in Manchester. In its original form its very *raison d'être* was to provide and improve transport in Greater Manchester and it alone would have the resources to investigate and initiate such a scheme. However, by the time the proposals were ready to be submitted to the Government the privatisation, which had become such a cornerstone of Conservative policy, had created a different situation.

In essence the crucial change which occurred was that the Government now required the light rail scheme to be funded by the private sector, and not from public money as would previously have been the case. Whatever the merits or otherwise of such a policy the results were to be far reaching. It became a condition of Government approval that private industry should design, build, operate and maintain the system (DBOM). Since the contractors were now being required to take commercial risks, and since they would also need to generate profits, it may be fairly assumed that the costs would increase.

Another vital factor was the financing of the £112m project. The Government had indicated that it would meet 50% of the remaining costs after the private sector contribution if the scheme met its criteria for a grant under Section 56 of the Transport Act of 1968, and without this grant the scheme would not be able to proceed.

The Consortium and the PTE prepared the massive documentation which eventually formed the Contract. There were so many documents that the signing alone took some 12 hours! Because there was so much documentation it was impossible to wait for it all to be completed and signed, and construction began six months before final Contracts were signed.

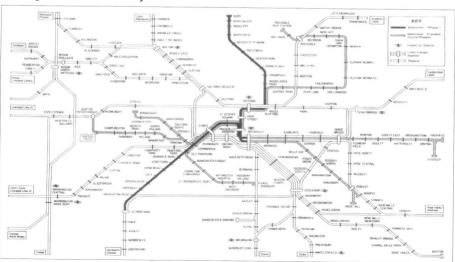

The Metrolink system as originally conceived. Note the similarities to the current network, even the operational links being the same. The only major change to the proposal is the replacement of the Glossop and Marple heavy rail lines by on-street running to Ashton-under-Lyne.

The Contract

In May 1988 the Greater Manchester Passenger Transport Authority, composed of elected members from each of the ten district authorities of Greater Manchester, invited 'suitable interested companies to apply for inclusion on a selected list of tenderers'. From over one hundred information packs issued, twelve consortia emerged as likely contenders to be considered for a Stage 1 tender listing and of these eight were selected to go forward to the next stage.

The concept of compiling a single contract to design, build, operate and maintain a light rail transit system in Great Britain was unique at the time, as was funding a passenger transportation project by a joint partnership of Government and private capital. The DBOM form of contract evolved after long consultations between the PTA and PTE and the Department of Transport, and provided for all the assets to remain in the ownership of the PTE. The Project Group of the PTE was charged with the responsibility for the tendering and evaluation of the Metrolink project. Three of the eight bidders later withdrew and five tenders were evaluated, the three eventually short-listed being the GMA Group, Norwest Holst/Hawker Siddeley and Trafalgar House/BREL.

For the second stage of the tender process the three consortia received additional data together with updated tender documentation, and they submitted their completed tenders in July 1989. On 7th September 1989, the contract for the design, building, operation and maintenance of the Greater Manchester Metrolink system was awarded to the GMA Consortium subject to the final approval of the Department of Transport.

On 24th October 1989, the then Minister of State for Transport, Mr Michael Portillo, announced that a grant under Section 56 of the Transport Act of 1968 would be available for the project, thus enabling the contract to proceed. The formal signing took place on 6th June 1990, itself a significant date and recalling the opening of the original Manchester Corporation tramway system on 6th June 1901. The contract was, in fact, in several parts which resulted in the signing session continuing into the night. All the elements of a DBOM contract between a PTE and a newly-established consortium, together with a funding package made up of elements from Central Government, the PTA and the contracting consortium added to the complexity of this unique form of contract.

The successful tenderer was initially known as the GMA Group, consisting of GEC Alsthom Transportation Projects Ltd, John Mowlem & Company PLC, and AMEC plc. GEC Alsthom was responsible directly or through its sub-contractors for the vehicles, the power supply system, signalling, telecommunications and the fare and ticketing systems. Similarly, Mowlem was responsible for the constructional work on the Cornbrook Viaduct, the G-Mex Viaduct and bowstring arch bridge over Great Bridgewater Street, stations, together with the construction of the city centre track and alignment. AMEC, through its subsidiary, Fairclough Civil Engineering Ltd, constructed the Operations and Maintenance Centre, consisting of the depot and offices at Queens Rd, Cheetham Hill,

Manchester. At the time of the tender, the GMA Group did not include a passenger transport operator. As it was considered essential that the successful consortium should include operating expertise, Greater Manchester Buses Ltd (GMBL), a company wholly owned by the PTA but subject to future privatisation, was appointed in November 1989, its financial contribution, *ie* its shareholding, allowing the purchase of a further light rail vehicle (LRV). The consortium, now including GMBL, formed a company with the title Greater Manchester Metro Ltd (GMML), which was incorporated in January 1990 to operate and maintain the system under contract to GMPTE.

The Operation and Maintenance Centre was constructed on former railway land on the site of the former Queens Road carriage sidings. During the conversion of the Bury line the contractors stored equipment and materials on the site, including the works train containing cement mixing and pole drilling equipment. The large building in the centre of the picture is the maintenance centre with the offices, staff quarters and control room in the foreground. The Bury line runs on viaduct across the back of the picture.
The business end of the Special Purpose Vehicle (SPV) is seen on the right.

The first phase

The first signs of Manchester Metrolink were seen when bus/rail interchanges were opened at Altrincham in 1978 and Bury in 1980. Phase One of Metrolink consisted of the conversion of the existing British Rail lines from Altrincham to Deansgate, and from Bury to Victoria. New light rail tracks were later laid in the city centre to connect the two with a spur branching off at Piccadilly Gardens into an interchange in the undercroft of Piccadilly station. New tram stops were provided at Victoria and Piccadilly railway stations and at G-Mex, Manchester's major exhibition centre converted from the former Central railway station, closed in 1969. The Piccadilly Station Interchange utilised part of the extensive clear area between the wide spans of the massive cast iron columns. New on-street stops were built in the city centre but elsewhere station refurbishment and Park and Ride provision was minimal to stay within the overall budget of £112 million which had kept the number of LRVs down to 25 (later 26), considerably restricting what could be done.

The Rail Strategy Study had assumed that on Intercity lines local British Rail services would continue to be provided by BR with financial support from the PTE. This left a number of lines carrying mainly or exclusively local services for which all or most of the costs would be borne by the PTE. These lines, receiving the heaviest subsidies, would be candidates for closure if severe constraints were to be applied to

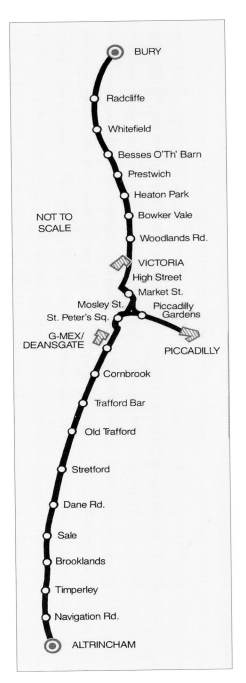

NOT TO SCALE

BURY
Radcliffe
Whitefield
Besses O'Th' Barn
Prestwich
Heaton Park
Bowker Vale
Woodlands Rd.
VICTORIA
High Street
Market St.
Mosley St.
St. Peter's Sq.
Piccadilly Gardens
G-MEX/ DEANSGATE
PICCADILLY
Cornbrook
Trafford Bar
Old Trafford
Stretford
Dane Rd.
Sale
Brooklands
Timperley
Navigation Rd.
ALTRINCHAM

revenue support and included those from Manchester to Bury, Altrincham, Oldham and Rochdale, Glossop and Hadfield and Marple and Rose Hill. All these lines met the criteria set by the study, namely that they must be capable of segregation from conventional heavy rail routes, they must be compatible with the development of the conventional rail network, existing or potential traffic must justify conversion to light rail, and the routes must contribute to a logical network and afford adequate interchange with the main BR network.

The Bury and Altrincham lines, however, possessed additional advantages. These lines entered Manchester from north and south respectively, they were the busiest lines of those under consideration, and each was outworn and outdated and would require considerable modernisation and re-equipment if they were to continue as heavy rail services.

The route of Phase One of Metrolink thus comprised three sections: the former railway between Bury and Victoria Station, the new city centre sections with a spur in the city centre from Piccadilly Gardens to Piccadilly Station and the rail alignment from G-Mex to Altrincham, representing a route length of 19.20 miles in total.

The original Bury and Altrincham lines were unlike most other suburban lines in Greater Manchester in that they were constructed primarily to serve local suburban journeys, especially for commuters, and for that reason are perhaps better located in relation to the development in those two corridors. This, no doubt, accounts for the relatively high passenger use which made them ideal candidates for conversion to light rail. The Bury line formed part of the original Lancashire and Yorkshire Railway but for over twenty years it operated independently of the rest of the British Rail network. This absence of interaction with other BR movements made conversion to light rail comparatively straightforward and less complicated.

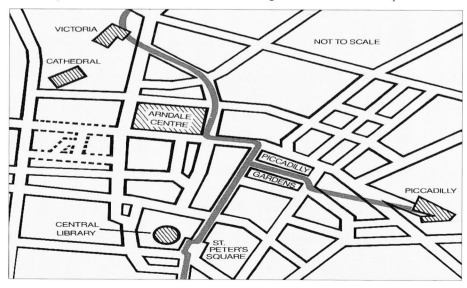

The Bury Line

The Manchester to Bury line was the first electric railway in the city. Originally opened by the Lancashire and Yorkshire Railway in 1879 it was electrified in 1916 on the side contact third rail system at 1200v dc. The original trains were of all-metal construction and are believed to have been the first of this type not only in Britain but probably in the world. From this modernity in 1916, the two-car EMUs latterly used had been built in 1959 and were 32 years old at the opening of Metrolink. Conversion of the obsolescent power system to 750v dc overhead, involved removal of the third rail and installation of the overhead catenary.

The northern terminus of the line is at Bury Interchange, opened in 1980, which replaced the former Bolton Street station. From Bury to Manchester Victoria the line is 9.86 miles long.

From the Interchange, adjacent to the pedestrianised shopping centre, the line heads southwards on former BR tracks through relatively open country, crossing the River Irwell before reaching Radcliffe where extensive park and ride facilities are provided. The line then re-crosses the Irwell by a lengthy viaduct and climbs steeply through a long cutting and a short tunnel to reach Whitefield station, also with a park and ride area.

After leaving Besses o'th Barn, the only intermediate island platform station, the line crosses the M62 Motorway on an unusual concrete structure of inverted T section as it heads for Prestwich and Heaton Park. The line then enters a cut and cover tunnel under the park, from which it emerges to reach Bowker Vale station.

Now within the leafy suburbs of North Manchester, Metrolink passes under Queens Road (where the city's first electric tramcar depot, opened in 1901, was built) near the branch to the first depot for the system, which is located on former BR sidings. A crossing of the Irk Valley and a tunnel at Collyhurst bring the line under Cheetham Hill Road bridge and into Victoria Station.

The nine existing stations on the line required some upgrading, with open access, automatic ticket vending machines, public address system and closed circuit TV surveillance monitored from the Control Centre at Queens Road.

Heaton Park station was typical of several on the Bury line where access to platforms could only be reached by long flights of steps from road level. New lifts were installed here to give easy access for everyone.

The Altrincham line

The line from the Altrincham Interchange to the former G-Mex Exhibition Centre forms the southern section of the route covering a distance of 7.66 miles. The route dates back to 1845, when it was authorised by the Manchester, South Junction and Altrincham Railway Act, opening for traffic in 1849. It was owned jointly by the LMS and LNER and the latter electrified it at 1500v dc overhead in 1931, killing off the parallel tram service at a stroke. Forty years later the line was converted to 25kV ac enabling British Railways to run its standard EMUs across the city and reduce congestion on the crowded South Junction line.

For Metrolink the Altrincham line was converted to 750v dc, making maximum use of the existing overhead equipment, but from Cornbrook Junction to G-Mex it runs along the viaduct which once served Central Station, requiring the erection of new catenary. There are, in fact, three parallel viaducts approaching G-Mex, the southerly former South Junction line, being used by British Railways, the central one by Metrolink and the northerly one currently disused.

At Cornbrook Junction a dive-under was built to take the Metrolink tracks beneath a re-aligned Warrington line before rejoining the original Altrincham route. Trafford Bar (formerly Old Trafford) station serves a run down inner city residential and commercial area, and Old Trafford (formerly Warwick Road) serves both the Lancashire County Cricket Ground and Manchester United Football Club.

The line then runs parallel to the Bridgewater Canal through Stretford for much of its journey to Altrincham, crossing over the River Mersey and under the M60 Motorway. Existing stations at Dane Road, Sale, Brooklands and Timperley link these residential areas to Manchester city centre.

South of Timperley there are two parallel single lines, one for Metrolink and one for BR. This is necessitated by the restricted width of the railway alignment between Deansgate Junction, where the BR tracks from Stockport join the Metrolink line, and Navigation Road. There are level crossings at Deansgate Lane and Navigation Road. South of Navigation Road reinstatement of two former goods loops provides a four-track formation enabling both BR and Metrolink to revert to double-track working. The line then passes under the A560 road to reach Altrincham Interchange, a four-platform station which remains in BR ownership, with two platforms for the heavy rail service between Manchester and Chester and two platforms for Metrolink. The latter are adjacent to the bus station in the former station courtyard which forms part of the interchange. This was the PTE's first major bus/rail interchange when opened in 1978.

As on the Bury line, the nine existing stations required refurbishing, and conversion where necessary to make them more open and accessible, being painted and signed in Metrolink corporate standard design. A new station at Cornbrook was later opened with a view to future development in the area, and as an interchange with the Eccles line.

The City Centre

Traffic congestion has been a problem in Manchester city centre for much of the past hundred years. Electric trams were no solution in their day as progress on fixed rail lines without segregation was easily blocked by other vehicles, notably horse-drawn traffic. The Rail Strategy Study defined a three-leg light rail route linking Victoria Station, the G-Mex Exhibition Centre and Piccadilly Station, partly segregated from other traffic, which would form the hub of a new light rail network.

Emerging from Victoria Station the line from Bury crossed Corporation Street into Balloon Street, then crossing Dantzic Street to Snow Hill which was the only area of significant demolition on the first phase of the system. This area is now occupied by the Shudehill tram stop and Transport Interchange which replaced the former Arndale bus station in what is now the city's Northern Quarter. Proceeding to High Street, the tracks run in the roadway, being segregated from other traffic. A tram stop was initially provided in High Street, towards Piccadilly, balanced by one in the opposite direction in Market Street, but further traffic management schemes have since enabled a two-way island platform to be provided at the latter point.

The line to Piccadilly railway station leaves the triangular junction to run alongside Piccadilly Gardens. The line then crosses Portland Street and runs down Aytoun Street before crossing London Road to enter the undercroft of Piccadilly Station, linked by escalators to the main concourse.

The third leg leaves the Piccadilly Gardens triangle to run down Mosley Street, which is restricted to trams and buses, into the stop at St Peter's Square outside the Central Library. Crossing Oxford Street it passes the Midland Hotel on segregated track, before joining the specially built ramped viaduct alongside the former G-Mex Exhibition Centre, now renamed 'Manchester Central'! Crossing Great Bridgewater Street by the striking bowstring bridge the line gains the former Cheshire Lines Committee railway alignment which it follows to Cornbrook.

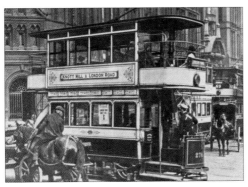

Traffic congestion in Manchester city centre is nothing new. This picture, taken about 1914, shows an early attempt by Manchester Corporation to provide an inter-station tram service between London Road and Central, but both termini were remote from the stations they purported to serve and it was little used for its original purpose. Even on the edge of the city centre the congestion is apparent.

Remarkably little demolition was needed to allow Metrolink to penetrate the key areas of the city. Snow Hill was the major exception. The line runs diagonally across the picture, the foreground now being occupied by the Shudehill transport interchange.

Piccadilly Undercroft provided the perfect interchange point between Metrolink and the Inter-City network, but the cost of creating the facility exceeded £2 million because British Railways' requirements meant a complete re-design. Major works included provision of concrete protection barriers around the cast iron columns supporting the main railway station and the installation of lifts and escalators.

Building Metrolink

With Government approval received for the scheme, work began in September 1989 at a number of different locations. Construction work on the Bury line was the more complex as it involved dismantling the old third rail system and erecting new masts and catenary. Relatively late in the proceedings a new overbridge was put in to allow access from the BR system to the privately owned East Lancashire Railway just south of Bury Interchange and a new connection had to be put in to allow access to the Queens Road depot and workshops. At Victoria new platforms were constructed and the line was re-aligned to allow it to swing out of the station onto the on-street section. In addition BR required substantial protection around the pillars supporting the roof.

Services to Bury from Manchester Victoria ceased on 13th July 1991, terminating from then on at Crumpsall. Complete withdrawal took place on 17th August just two weeks short of the line's 112th Anniversary, after which a rail replacement bus service operated.

British Rail also required very high levels of protection within Victoria Station. Some of the massive concrete barriers can be seen here in course of construction. The location created one of the sharpest curves on the system which still would benefit from flange lubrication to reduce squeal and wear.

By contrast the Altrincham line required the least change. The BR track and catenary was already in place and was compatible with light rail transit. Construction work was largely concerned with conversion of the electrical current from 25kV ac to 750v dc and installation of separate LRT signalling. An early complication was that part of the Altrincham line carried diesel multiple units on the BR route between Manchester and Chester. However, from May 1989 these services were diverted to use the freight line between Altrincham and Stockport.

While the track and overhead system was relatively straightforward to prepare, the line required four major items of construction work: the creation of a turnback siding immediately south of Timperley station, an underpass at Cornbrook Junction, the complete refurbishment of Cornbrook viaduct and the construction of the G-Mex viaduct which is dealt with later. The new underpass was necessary to separate the line from Manchester Piccadilly and Oxford Road to Warrington, with 25kV overhead to Trafford Park Containerbase, from the 750v dc Metrolink line. Metrolink passes under the BR line at this point and the design allowed for a possible extension to Salford Quays and Trafford Park to be constructed some time in the future.

Cornbrook viaduct was originally built between 1876 and 1878 by the Midland Railway, and carried two tracks into the former Central Station which, despite its name was, like the others in Manchester, on the edge of the city centre. The approach was increased in the 1890s by a further three tracks when a new viaduct was constructed to the northern side of the railway leading into the Great Northern Railway's goods station. From 1969, following the closure of Central Station, the Cornbrook viaduct was disused with little or no maintenance work being carried out. As a result the metal sections had become corroded and the brickwork had decayed. An extensive repair programme was carried out including the replacement of one metal-deck bridge. This viaduct is unusual in that it divides into two independent structures at which point Metrolink uses the southern portion.

Construction work on the nine existing stations on the Altrincham line included disabled access by the provision of new or modified access ramps and, where ramps were not appropriate, the installation of lifts monitored from the Control Centre. Station bridges, retaining walls and platforms were brought up to standard, and the construction work also included the provision of new ducts and building services and new prefabricated buildings or the modification of existing buildings to suit the requirements of LRT passengers. At the same time fencing and lighting was upgraded and Metrolink standard signing was introduced, together with the installation of public address and information display systems.

A number of options for the route in the city centre were contained in the Rail Study. Having examined all the relevant factors, particularly the effect that light rail operation would have on other traffic movements including those of buses and pedestrians, the present route was defined.

A significant aspect of construction in the city centre concerned the public utilities; electricity, gas, water and telephone, the underground pipes and cables all of which would be affected by the track work. To avoid costly and disruptive subsequent repair work all services under or adjacent to the track bed were re-routed, the work having to be carried out before construction began. By judicious diversion of traffic flows and other traffic management schemes it was possible to segregate much of the route from general traffic.

Track laying began in 1991, the first stage being to break out the existing road surface and dig out the underlying base. The excavation was bottomed out and a thin layer of blinding concrete laid to form a clean working surface. Steel reinforcing mesh was then laid and the concrete foundation poured on top of it. The steel mesh not only provides support, but also acts as a conductor drawing off any stray current. A latex and cement screed was then laid to a level 25mm below the base of the rail and topped off with a final pour of concrete.

The next process was rail laying proper. The rails, manufactured in Luxembourg, were delivered as straight section and bent to shape on site. Once aligned and levelled the rails were embedded in a polymer adhesive to maintain track geometry without tie bars and to insulate against noise, vibration and electrical leakage and then welded on site. It would be true to say that new technology and old fashioned wet Manchester conspired to create severe problems and a long learning curve ensued. Nowadays the rail can be supplied pre-encapsulated. The pointwork was prefabricated at Balfour Beatty's Sandiacre works ready to be dropped into place as complete units. Finally the road surface was reinstated.

The city centre includes varying degrees of segregation from on-street running with other traffic to private right of way, with partial segregation where the alignment is shared with local buses or access traffic. Six tram stops were required on the city

An Altrincham-bound train approaches Cornbrook Junction while to the left track laying for Metrolink proceeds on the adjoining viaduct. This is the point at which the ramp from the Cornbrook underpass joins the viaduct leading to G-Mex.

The track base takes shape in Nicholas Croft with shuttering in place above the blinding layer and the metal mesh laid over concrete spacer blocks. Note the service pipes crossing the track bed providing for a source of future revenue.

centre section, not including Victoria and Piccadilly. The stops have side platforms except for Piccadilly Gardens which has a single island platform. G-Mex (now Deansgate-Castlefield) had staggered platforms either side of the crossing leading from the footbridge to Deansgate and the Manchester Central Exhibition Centre. Major requirements of tram stop design were that they should be as unobtrusive as possible and ensure maximum accessibility for the disabled. Platforms incorporate distinct and attractive waiting shelters and a central information area including ticket vending machines, route maps and signing.

The major construction project on the Altrincham line was the ramp alongside Lower Mosley Street and the bowstring bridge over Great Bridgewater Street which is regarded as part of the city centre. This wholly new structure carries Metrolink from street level at Windmill Street to the tram stop on the viaduct at the former Central Station throat. Construction

June 1991 and the delta junction on Mosley Street is taking shape. The branch to Piccadilly Station diverges here while the former Lewis's store stands at the left side of the picture.

of the viaduct required the provision of a new retaining wall running its full length. The wall and the viaduct itself are formed of reinforced concrete. In order that they should blend with the existing structures it was a requirement that brick cladding should be added to the exterior.

The steel bowstring arch bridge crossing Great Bridgewater Street was designed to reflect its surroundings. The diamond shape of the roof lights of the G-Mex building is repeated in the arch of the bridge and the square section of the box arch has been turned on its side to present a diamond shape. The bridge, like others on the system, was painted in the aquamarine colour scheme used throughout the Metrolink system at the time, now mostly replaced by yellow. The polymer system was used for securing the rails on the bridge to reduce noise, which is important on bridges of this design and especially so with its proximity to the Exhibition Hall and the Bridgewater Concert Hall at either side, the latter occupying the site of the former Lower Mosley Street bus station.

This major construction project was carefully devised to be sympathetic with the Victorian brick structure of the original Central Station and the design was approved by the Royal Fine Arts Commission.

A notable landmark in the city is the fine bowstring bridge erected in 1991 which enables Metrolink cars to cross Great Bridgewater Street on to the former railway viaduct leading to Cornbrook and the South Manchester lines. The former Central station is behind and the ramp down to street level and the Midland Hotel are in the background. The factory-made, pre-formed brick panels have not yet been fitted to the right hand descending section.

The vehicles

Metrolink's specially designed trams were purpose built by the Firema Consortium in Italy, each consisting of two similar cars connected by an articulation unit supported by the centre bogie. By this means the 29 metre long units could negotiate a minimum radius of 25 metres, necessary for some of the sharp curves in the city, particularly those at Market Street and High Street.

Because the cars had to cope with two quite different boarding situations; on-street and from existing railway station platforms, much thought was given to the best and most appropriate design. A further important requirement was to provide access for disabled persons in wheelchairs, and also for passengers with children in pushchairs or with heavy luggage.

Whilst a low-floor design would have made entry from the street easy, the existence of the 18 railway stations mitigated against this. It was finally decided to construct small on-street stations, with a section of the platforms at the same height as the railway station platforms. However, this was not very satisfactory and most platforms were later raised to full height throughout their length. A further later proposal to insert a third, low level, car in the middle of each unit was considered to be impractical.

The nominal capacity of each articulated unit was 201 passengers, of whom 86 were seated. In peak conditions 270 could be carried. It was a part of the philosophy that passengers should be able to stand in the vehicle, if need be, whilst travelling rather than at the station waiting for a train running to a less frequent timetable.

Because the height, degree of slope and general appearance of the on-street station platforms were recognised as being critical if the objectives of maximum access and aesthetic appeal were to be achieved, a mock-up was constructed and exhibited during the Autumn of 1988 in the then disused Birchfields Road bus depot. Almost four decades previously the city's last tram had made its fateful journey into this same depot when the original tramway system closed on the morning of January 10th 1949. The mock-up was set against a profiled platform to a modified design and allowed detailed examination of many aspects of the car's design to be made and also provided a useful forum for discussion with the many interested groups of people who needed or wanted to see the vehicle.

The mock-up car allowed evaluation of the ramped platforms and access to the vehicle.

To assist everyone involved in the project it was subsequently arranged for a prototype body shell to be delivered to Manchester in March 1990 and housed in one of the arches under the main line railway into Piccadilly station. It later found a home in the Greater Manchester Museum of Transport.

The availability of this prototype helped in other ways. The interior of the cars had been designed in consultation with Metrolink's future passengers, some 2,000 of whom visited the prototype during the several days when it was available to everyone for inspection and comment, following which many minor modifications were made.

Both the interior and exterior of the cars had been designed to give a modern attractive appearance and also to be capable of being easily kept clean and serviced. Design Consultants were involved in devising the Metrolink corporate identity and colour scheme, the livery for the vehicles and the overall styling both inside and out helped in other ways. The interior of the cars used modern materials to reduce maintenance to a minimum and also to meet stringent safety regulations. An automatic car washing plant was installed at Queens Road to wash every car once every 24 hours. The 26 two-car articulated LRVs were built by the Firema Consortium, under contract to GEC Alsthom (GECA). All five factories in the consortium, at Bologna, Cittadella, two in Caserta, and Padua were involved in the work. GECA, in addition to its on-site engineer, also had a team of its electrical specialists at each factory. The bogies for all 26 cars included wheelsets and axles from Germany and motors from GECA at Preston.

The first vehicle was dispatched by road from Bologna on 23rd July. Its journey was not uneventful. Italian and French police held

The first vehicle is rolled out at Bologna, still incomplete but ready for bogie clearance testing. Metrolink's Operations Director watches progress over the points with a keen eye.

it up during peak holiday times and when it finally arrived on British soil it demolished one of the escorting BMW police cars whilst ably demonstrating the extreme manoeuvrability of its purpose-built trailer.

Following arrival at Queens Road on 29th August the delicate and difficult job of unloading took place next day. A gently sloping ramp had been constructed and brought over on the towing vehicles. The complete vehicle was rolled off the low loading trailer and down the ramp and coupled, via the Dellner coupling, to the Metrolink SPV diesel locomotive. It was then moved into the workshops for commissioning by GECA staff before being handed over to GMML for staff training to begin.

In view of the urgency to get further vehicles to GMML for staff training and familiarisation consideration was even given to air freighting at least two further vehicles using the Soviet-built Antonov aircraft which could accommodate two Metrolink vehicles, although this option was not taken up.

Metrolink's first unit sweeps majestically along the M6 on its way to Manchester, with the necessary police Land Rover escort tucked safely away at the very back, while below it stands outside the Metrolink headquarters at Queens Road waiting to be offloaded in front of the Glossop company's video camera.

Testing the route

Now that the first cars had arrived a start could be made on testing the route for clearances. The first car made its all-important gauging run through the city in the early hours of Sunday 15th September 1991, when unit 1001 was propelled by Metrolink's Special Purpose Vehicle (SPV) from Queens Road to Victoria Station, where it remained whilst the SPV diesel ran to Aytoun Street and back. The convoy then made its way to St Peter's Square where the SPV carried on to G-Mex and back, before both vehicles were taken over the various legs of the Delta junction. The trial was successful and the way was clear to complete the work ready for the system opening early the following year.

The gauging convoy stands in High Street opposite the Arndale Centre and, below, unit 1001 poses in St Peter's Square waiting the return of the SPV. Overhead wiring has yet to begin in the square.

24

The maintenance area in the Queens Road workshops is spacious and well equipped with doors at either end allowing vehicles to pass through the building. The SPV and flat truck are standing on one of the pit roads, one of which incorporates a wheel lathe at rail height, allowing turning to take place without removing wheels and axles from the bogies.

Control and Signalling

Metrolink's headquarters, where its offices, staff facilities, control centre, depot sidings, washing plant and workshops were situated, formed an £8 million four hectare brand new purpose built complex built on the former Manchester Loop line immediately south of the bridge carrying Queens Road over the Bury line. At the time it was opened it provided all the necessary facilities to service, clean and maintain the whole fleet, the workshop being fully equipped with pits and a wheel lathe. In addition, Metrolink's diesel shunting locomotive, the SPV, was based here.

The complex also housed the nerve centre of the whole Metrolink operation, the Control Centre, controlling vehicles, signals and power distribution, with three visual display units (VDUs) enabling the whole operation to be monitored and controlled from one room. The Control Centre is manned 24 hours a day, 365 days a year. For the first phase there were three people manning Control with responsibility for monitoring the tram service, surveillance of stations, control of power supplies, monitoring of ticket machines and supervision of staff.

The Control Centre monitors the running of the service to ensure that trams are running to time and to take remedial action when they are not. This is done on a 'by exception' basis where it assumed that everything is running to plan unless it is seen to be otherwise. Monitoring services also includes dealing with emergencies. These may be mishaps on the system itself, such as accidents, or external such as an incident in the city centre. For such eventualities there are hot lines to the emergency services control rooms.

All Metrolink stations are unmanned but are under closed circuit television (CCTV) surveillance. They are polled on a regular basis and the picture comes up on one of the 14 VDU screens in the Control Centre. Cameras monitor the platforms, ticket vending machines (TVM) and subways. All stations have public address and stations can be called individually, in groups or system-wide. Public announcements are used only during out-of-course running or when emergencies arise. Real time displays are now in use.

On each platform there is a Passenger Emergency Call (PEC) button which enables a passenger to talk direct to the Controller. Pressing this button also brings the relevant camera picture onto the screen so that the Controller can both see and talk to the passenger.

The receipt of power from the supplier and its distribution across the system both for traction and other purposes is also monitored by Control and any section of Metrolink can be isolated if the need arises.

All TVMs are monitored. If anything goes wrong, from running out of change to a complete failure, it is reported for corrective action to be taken. All TVMs are fitted with an alarm in case of their being attacked or vandalised. Although staff duty rosters are known well in advance there may be a need to revise these rosters on an *ad hoc* basis.

Original design of ticket vending machine at Bowker Vale station on the Bury Line.

In BR days the level crossing at Hagside between Bury and Radcliffe used to be controlled from a small signal box. As part of the conversion to Metrolink it is now under the supervision of the Control Centre. The crossing barriers lower automatically on the approach of the train but the signal protecting the crossing is cleared by the Controller when he can see, through the CCTV monitor, that there is nothing trapped on the crossing. The barriers are equipped with 'auto-rise' and 'second train coming' facilities.

For the first phase of Metrolink two different types of signalling were used. The segregated former railway sections were fully signalled with a two-aspect automatic system incorporating the latest Solid State Interlocking (SSI) technology. A station warning board was positioned at braking distance before each station and yellow/green distance signals were used where the sighting of the normal red/green signals was restricted, and automatic train stops were provided to stop any tram passing a signal at red.

In an emergency, vehicles can be turned back at G-Mex and Victoria enabling each line to operate a shuttle service should the city centre section be blocked. Units can also be stabled in sidings at Timperley and Victoria, as well as the platforms at Bury and Altrincham and the headshunt at Sheffield Street. Crossovers were installed at Whitefield, Crumpsall, Old Trafford, Aytoun Street and London Road, but those at Old Trafford and London Road were later removed. The single line section on the Altrincham line is under the control of the BR signal box at Deansgate Lane.

In the city centre the driver drives 'on sight', as would any other road user. Here he is in sole charge and has full responsibility for the safe progress of the vehicle. The design of the signals for street running Light Rail Transit was discussed by a working party made up from representatives of the Railway Inspectorate, the Department of Transport and traffic signal engineers from Manchester and Sheffield. Sheffield's Supertram system was, of course, also under construction at this time. To use conventional traffic lights would have risked causing confusion to other drivers, so the preferred solution was a white bar symbol as used on several European systems. Here a single aspect signal displays a horizontal bar for stop and a vertical one for go. Diagonal bars indicate turn left or turn right.

The points at the delta junction in Piccadilly are automatically set for an approaching vehicle, depending on a route code entered by the driver at the start of each journey into the vehicle's electronic recognition system, points indicators enabling the drivers to check that the points are set correctly. All points have provision for heating in icy weather.

New two-aspect colour light signalling being installed north of Bowker Vale during the conversion of the Bury line. A BR lookout man stands by while a Bury to Victoria train passes. The mouth of Heaton Park tunnel can be seen in the background.

Dressed in Metrolink aquamarine, HM Queen Elizabeth II officially opens the system at a ceremony in St Peter's Square on 17th July 1992. She is pictured with Councillor Jack Flanagan on the left and Councillor Joe Clarke, Chairman of GMPTA. After the ceremony the official party left for Bury on a special tram.

The system opens

Although the official opening was not until 17th July 1992, Metrolink had in fact been carrying fare-paying passengers for some weeks prior to that date. The Bury to Victoria Station section had opened on 6th April when cars 1004 and 1008, coupled together as a double unit, worked the 0600 departure from Bury Interchange. At the same time car 1012 left Victoria travelling in the opposite direction. Commemorative first-day tickets were sold in advance, allowing the holder unlimited travel between Bury and Victoria all that day for the price of £3.50. On the first day of operation some 11,000 journeys were made, but it settled down to something like half of this after the novelty had worn off. Nevertheless this was a strong base for growth and passenger numbers rose steadily.

The important on-street section from Victoria to G-Mex opened to the public three weeks later on 27th April when car number 1007 broke a ceremonial tape as it moved along the streets carrying officials and members of the press and public. With direct access to the city centre ridership soared, capacity loads being carried. The G-Mex to Altrincham section was linked into the system on 15th June when trams started running through between Altrincham and Bury, and phase one was completed with the opening of the Piccadilly spur on 20th July, three days after the official opening.

METROLINK
Price £3.50
Commemorative Issue
Sponsored by Bury Times Newspaper Group
Ticket design by students of Bury College
Issue No. 030884
Valid on the first day of commercial operation between Bury and G-Mex Stations

A Bury-bound tram stands in the new Metrolink platforms at Victoria Station soon after the opening of the first stage.

Tram number 1007 runs through the commemorative banner at High Street stop to open the Victoria to G-Mex section on 15th July 1992. Number 1007 was chosen for the ceremony as it was also the number of the Manchester Corporation tram which operated the last journey on Monday 10th January 1949. It has now been put aside for preservation.

Bury Interchange was opened on 17th March 1980 at a cost of £4.9 million, replacing the town's former Bolton Street station, which is now used by the preserved East Lancashire Railway. The station opens off the main bus station concourse and passengers pass a row of ticket vending machines on the left before descending escalators to the island platform. A lift is also provided.

On the left unit number 1022 is seen leaving the Interchange on its way to Altrincham. The bridge in the background, once the former British Railways Rochdale to Bolton line, now carries the East Lancashire Railway across the Metrolink tracks.

South of Bury is Hagside, one of three level crossings on the Bury to Altrincham line. Formerly controlled by the signal box on the left, it is now automatically operated and supervised by the Control Centre at Old Trafford.

Whitefield, three miles south of Bury, rapidly became the busiest intermediate station on the route. Here unit number 1017 emerges from Whitefield tunnel and runs into the inward bound platform, while number 1026 prepares to leave the opposite platform for Bury. Whitefield was initially little changed apart from de-roofing the steps down to the platform.

Immediately beyond the island platform at Besses o'th' Barn the line runs on to the viaduct straddling Bury Old Road and the M60 motorway in one uninterrupted span. Built for British Railways in 1969, the Metrolink tracks are carried either side of a single concrete girder.

In the bottom picture tram number 1006 arrives at Bowker Vale station. Built in concrete in the art deco style, when it opened in the 1930s it must have seemed strikingly modern, but the years have not been kind. The footbridge has since lost its roof and the rest of the buildings have recently been demolished and replaced by Metrolink standard shelters.

Initially Crumpsall retained its 1980s station buildings and covered staircases. It was one of the first stations on the system to be converted to a simple tram stop, the booking hall being demolished and replaced by a pair of ticket vending machines, the stairs being de-roofed and lifts provided.

The former halt at Woodlands Road was built on a high embankment making access difficult. It was replaced by new stops either side at Abraham Moss and Queens Road, which are more accessible and serve the area better. A double unit is seen below at Abraham Moss in April 2011.

Metrolink's Queens Road depot and workshops were built on the site of the former Queens Road carriage sidings on the disused loop line between Victoria and Thorp's Bridge junction. Above, car number 1004 coasts down hill from Irk Valley viaduct toward the staff halt where driver changeovers take place. The new Queens Road tram stop is now being built on this site. After leaving Victoria Station trams cross Corporation Street and travel up Balloon Street between the Co-operative Group Offices. Balloon Street is now restricted to trams and the limited amount of road traffic requiring access to the Co-op premises. After crossing Dantzig Street the line runs into Snow Hill, now the site of the Shudehill tram stop, part of the new transport interchange opened in January 2006, situated on the vacant land at the bottom right of the picture.

At first Metrolink shared Market Street with buses and the tram stop was one-way towards Victoria, being balanced by stops in High Street and Mosley Street in the opposite direction. Unit number 1006 is seen above on a Bury working before the new island platform was built. The picture clearly shows the complicated arrangement for mixed-level loading originally used.

From Piccadilly Gardens the route passes along Aytoun Street before crossing waste ground which later became the Piccadilly Place development and London Road before disappearing into the undercroft of Piccadilly main line station.
In the lower picture a Bury-bound tram loads passengers in the departure platform.

A busy scene in St Peter's Square as buses give right of way to a Metrolink unit. Both modes of transport then share the northbound lane up Mosley Street. In the lower picture the photographer gets a panoramic view of the city as an Altrincham-bound tram breasts the ramp from street level and runs alongside the Exhibition Centre towards G-Mex station. The car park in the right background is now the Bridgewater Concert Hall, home of Manchester's Hallé Orchestra.

From G-Mex the line runs along the former Midland Railway viaduct through an area of derelict industry which is steadily being developed into up-market canal-side housing. An Altrincham-bound service is seen above approaching the new Cornbrook station which was designed as an interchange with the proposed Eccles line and initially had no external access.

Old Trafford station on the corner of Seymour Grove and Talbot Road was renamed Trafford Bar, more accurately to reflect its true location adjacent to the old toll bar. The original Victorian booking office stands unused and boarded up, access to the platforms now being by staircases and ramps from the surrounding streets.

One station little changed was Brooklands, work consisting of removing the separate footbridge from the redundant booking office and replacing it by access to the stairs direct from Marsland Road. "The Brook" public house on the outward platform is named after Samuel Brook, a local industrialist who was instrumental in establishing the station in the 1850s.

Between Deansgate Lane and Navigation Road there are two parallel single tracks, one for Metrolink and the other for Network Rail's Stockport to Chester line, each with its own bi-directional platform. A lengthy coal train for Fiddlers Ferry Power Station is seen passing through the station. At Altrincham Metrolink services use the two bay platforms next to the booking office and the interchange. Work is here progressing on refurbishing the Victorian cast iron canopy.

The Eccles Line

With the first line up and running, attention then turned to expanding the network. The Metrolink 2000 plan had included a line to serve Salford Quays, Greater Manchester's equivalent of London's Docklands. There were to have been two routes leaving the Altrincham line at Cornbrook and splitting at Pomona, a northern leg crossing the ship canal and running through the former dock area to a terminus at Broadway, and the other keeping to the southern bank through Trafford Park, crossing the canal to the west of Eccles to an interchange with the Manchester to Liverpool railway line near Barton Airport and on the way serving the proposed huge retail and leisure complex which would later become the Trafford Centre. The intention was to act as a catalyst for rebuilding the derelict docks and to breathe new life into the declining heavy industrial area of Trafford Park.

The branch was to be funded largely by private capital, primarily from Peel Holdings, the owners of the Trafford Centre and much of Trafford Park, but this was linked to building a second complex on the other side of the motorway. Planning permission was not forthcoming so the line was not built. A further branch to the Lowry Centre was also mooted, again to be funded by private capital, which again did not materialise, although a junction and crossover was laid in west of Harbour City which would later be used for the short branch to MediaCityUK. Parliamentary powers were granted for the truncated proposal in 1990.

Having lost out by the abandonment of the original proposal, political pressure from Salford Council for a service to serve Eccles resulted in further powers being sought for an extension of the Broadway line through to Eccles, these being granted in 1995.

The branch opened as far as Broadway on 6th December 1999 and to Eccles on 21st July 2000. The line leaves the Altrincham route by a flying junction immediately south of Cornbrook and runs on a new viaduct between the Ship Canal and the former Cheshire Lines Committee Liverpool line. The first station is at Pomona, an island platform on the new viaduct named after the now derelict Pomona Docks nearby. At the platform end the line turns sharp right to cross the Ship Canal. Provision was made here for the projected Trafford Park branch. The line then threads its way through the new development of the Quays before reaching the one-time temporary terminus at Broadway. From here the route is on public road along South Langworthy Road and Eccles New Road to Ladywell where an underpass takes it into the centre of Eccles.

Because of the on-street running between Broadway and Eccles the six new cars ordered for the line had to be to a modified specification. The original cars were unable to run through to Eccles as legislation relating to trams on street had been changed since 1992. They now needed retractable couplers, fenders and bogie skirts, and the braking system had to be revised. Most of the older cars were rebuilt to the modified specification to allow operational flexibility.

At Pomona the Eccles line turns sharp right to cross the Manchester Ship Canal by a spectacular single span bridge. Provision has already been made for the proposed line to the Trafford Centre and Port Salford which will go straight on. The Liverpool railway line is on the left.

In the upper picture an Eccles-bound tram has just left Salford Quays stop and is approaching Toronto Drive. Ontario Basin is on the right. Most of the roads in the Quays have Canadian names after the places served by Manchester Liners which sailed mainly between Manchester and the Great Lakes ports. The cranes stood there from 1988 until October 2013 when, having served as a reminder of the importance of the former dockland, they were demolished as dangerous and beyond economic repair.

In the centre a tram rounds the corner from the Broadway stop on its way to Piccadilly. In the distance an Eccles-bound unit stands in Harbour City stop with the massive Erie Basin apartment block rising behind. In the foreground is the turn out for the planned single line branch to the Lowry Centre.

Journey's end at Eccles in the lower view as a tram rests in the sunshine before heading back to Piccadilly.

The Big Bang

The original plan had always seen the initial Metrolink system as a springboard for a much larger network, including the conversion of selected British Rail suburban lines to light rail operation. This continued to be the basis for all future planning although the detail would change.

Prime Minister John Major came to Manchester in September 1992 to discuss the future of the system with members of the Passenger Transport Authority and the operating consortium, including funding and extensions to the network. He rode from Victoria to Bury and drove the tram for part of the journey.

The following year the Executive published its proposals to extend the existing network to South Manchester and the Airport, to Rochdale via Oldham and to Ashton-under-Lyne, with a further two lines to the Lowry Centre and Trafford Park, subject to obtaining private sector funding. These proposals were submitted to the Government in July 1998 and Parliamentary Powers were obtained during 1999. The project became known officially as Metrolink 2000, or more popularly as the 'Big Bang'.

In July 2000, at the official opening of the Phase 2 Eccles extension, the then Transport Minister Bev Hughes announced that a £326 million funding package had been agreed between the Government and the Greater Manchester authorities, the remainder of the £500 million estimated cost being secured from private sector contributions. Work then commenced on the planning and letting of contracts.

With Government approval, land was acquired and property demolished, and new infrastructure was built. By the spring of 2003 a 75-metre tunnel had been built to reach the Manchester Airport Ground Transport Interchange and an underpass had been constructed under Alan Turing Way on the Ashton line. Soon afterwards the futuristic new station at Central Park and the spectacular curving flyover to carry the Rochdale tracks over the main railway line to Yorkshire at Thorp's Bridge were completed.

Everything was going well, but in July 2004 the Government, alarmed by the costs spiralling out of control, called a halt to the scheme. At the time Prime Minister Tony Blair said that projected costs had doubled and, while the original amount promised was still available, the remainder would have to be found elsewhere before work could proceed. This resulted in public outrage across the region amid accusations that the money was to be diverted to fund projects in London and it took two years of intensive lobbying and the threat of claims for millions of pounds of compensation for the work already done, before the Government agreed a compromise.

On 6th July 2006 Transport Secretary Douglas Alexander announced that a new package had been put in place to allow partial implementation of Phase 3. Officially dubbed Phase 3A, or more commonly the 'Little Bang', this generally comprised routes on existing track bed while, with the exception of the politically sensitive Ashton line, deferring construction of the more expensive on-street sections for an unspecified period.

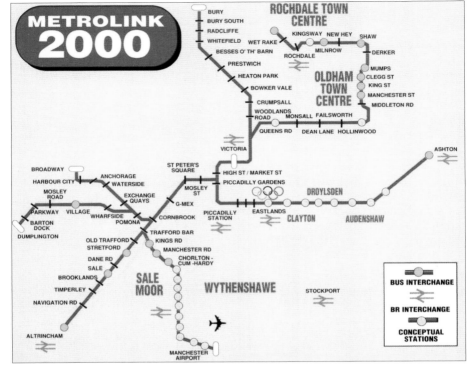

Metrolink 2000, or the Big Bang, as originally planned.

Work restarted immediately on the scheme as follows:-

- A branch to serve the MediaCityUK complex in Salford Quays, funded by the North West Regional Development Agency and the University of Salford.
- The South Manchester line as far as St Werburgh's Road, Chorlton.
- The East Manchester line as far as Droylsden.
- The Rochdale line as far as Rochdale Railway Station and omitting on-street running in Oldham and Rochdale.

- A second depot at Old Trafford.
- Forty new trams and new fares collection equipment.
- A new yellow and silver colour scheme.

Then in July 2006 a special £1.5 billion funding package was agreed for transport schemes in Greater Manchester that would allow more of the original package to be completed, initially the extensions from Chorlton to East Didsbury, from Droylsden to Ashton and into Rochdale and Oldham town centres, with a target date of 2014 and eventually to Manchester Airport by 2016.

In September 1992 Prime Minister John Major met members of the Passenger Transport Authority to discuss the future expansion of Metrolink. During his visit he drove unit number 1002, named 'Manchester Arndale Voyager', for a short distance. The picture shows him inspecting the controls at Bowker Vale station before starting off. Afterwards Mr Major remarked that he had enjoyed the experience and that it was the best train set he had ever played with.

At Bury he was presented with a copy of the first Metrolink handbook by Geoffrey Senior on behalf of the publishers.

A new Railway

Apart from simply extending the network, the Big Bang included modernising the existing system with new trams, new signalling, a second depot at Old Trafford, new ticket vending machines and a complete makeover of Metrolink's corporate image with new logo and new yellow and grey colour scheme. In addition, Metrolink also instituted a rolling programme to upgrade the original system, bringing it up to date with current light rail standards and all the latest legislation regarding disability access. This effectively meant the launching of a brand new railway.

With self-service ticketing, the opportunity was taken to provide open access from as much of the surrounding area as possible, with ramps for prams and wheelchairs or, where this was not possible, lifts as well. For security all stations would be well lit and there would also be CCTV surveillance and a passenger alarm system. On the Rochdale route, converted from a former heavy rail line, a completely new railway was created on the old track bed, all the stations being demolished and replaced with new state-of-the-art tram stops.

New Trams

The original system had used a fleet of 32 trams, 26 of class T68 for the Bury and Altrincham lines (1001-26) and six similar cars of class T68A for Eccles (2001-6). The T68 cars could not operate on the Eccles line, so a number of units had been modified to give a degree of operational flexibility, effectively producing a third design. For the additional work resulting from the extended system a total of 40 new trams was ordered from Bombardier. These were its Flexity Swift M5000 model, basically to a design in widespread use across the Continent as well as on the Croydon Tramlink. They were built at Bombardier's plant in Vienna with electrical equipment by Kiepe of Dusseldorf.

The tram is a two-section articulated vehicle carried on three bogies with a maximum speed of 80 kmh (50 mph) with a driver's cab at each end and a central-mounted pantograph. At 39.7 tonnes each unit is 10 tonnes lighter than the T68s with consequently less wear and tear on the track and other components, although this tends to show on the fast, open stretches of the system, notably the former BR track between Bury and Radcliffe. An additional batch of eight was ordered in 2007 with an option to increase this to 97. Initially this rose to 62, but the older trams were now showing their age and needing costly refurbishment, especially to the floors, so a decision was made to replace them and benefit from the economies of running a single homogenous fleet. The total currently stands at 94.

Old Trafford Depot

The depot and workshops at Queens Road were built with room for further expansion, so additional sidings were added and a second entry provided from the Rochdale line utilising the track bed of the former Manchester Loop under the Bury line from Smedley Viaduct Junction, enabling trams from that direction to enter or leave the depot without complicated reversal. However, it soon became clear that, due to site constraints, it would not be possible to accommodate all the additional vehicles at Queens Road, so it was decided to build a second depot at Old Trafford on a derelict site in the V between the Altrincham and South Manchester lines just west of Trafford Bar Station.

The new depot was opened in 2011 and covers an area of some 67,000 square metres. It includes workshop and office space, a tram washing plant and extensive stabling sidings which were initially used to store and carry out commissioning of the new trams before they went into service and now house withdrawn T68 units awaiting disposal. The Control Centre also moved there from Queens Road.

Tram Management

The signalling on stage one was a simple automatic two-aspect system on the reserved sections of the line, with on-sight running on street. This sufficed for the frequencies then involved, but was impracticable for the greatly reduced headways resulting from the Big Bang; also the equipment was now some 20 years old with increasing maintenance costs and decreasing reliability. So it was decided to institute a new Tram Management System. This essentially extends line-of-sight to the whole system, but at places where this is too short or there are conflicting movements such as approaching junctions, lineside signalling is provided. Every tram has an on-board computer which relays exact information on its route, location and speeds to the system and enables the central computer to set the signals appropriately.

The complexity of the system and

problems with interface with the existing lines such as at Irk Valley Junction and Trafford Bar caused problems which required a temporary solution resulting in delays to the implementation of the new routes.

Ticket Machines

With the expanded system new state-of-the-art ticket machines were introduced. These have easy to use touch screens and give a choice of several languages and a number of different ways to pay. Passengers can also buy daily, 4-weekly, quarterly or annual season tickets. At busy locations 'Queue Busters' are provided, issuing only on-the-day single or return tickets.

Corporate Livery

When the system opened in 1992, a corporate livery of aquamarine, grey and white was devised including a stylised M logo. For the relaunch a completely new livery was produced featuring a pale yellow and grey colour scheme and a diamond motif formed from a pattern of diminishing circles which was applied to signage and publicity. The tram livery features yellow cab ends blending into grey sides with black doors. It was originally intended to paint the older trams into the new colours, but with the decision to withdraw these early, only one unit (number 1003) was so treated.

Above, a pair of M5000 units stand face to face at Bury Interchange, displaying the yellow and grey livery.

The view on the left of the Monsall tram stop on the Rochdale line, taken from Jocelyn Street bridge, shows to perfection the layout of the modern purpose-built structure with its open access from the surrounding streets by ramps, stairs and a lift. A new tram leaves the stop on a driver training duty the week before the service opened to the public.

On the right lines of trams awaiting commissioning stand outside the Old Trafford workshops, while below new ticket vending machines, a customer telephone and alarm and an information panel are in the corporate livery at the MediaCityUK terminus.

The City Centre

The condition of the track leading from Aytoun Street past the new PTE headquarters.

More immediately urgent was the condition of the track in the city centre. So during the summer of 2009 the entire section between St Peter's Square and Victoria was closed so that the track could be completely renewed and the tram stops upgraded to cater for the increase in traffic that the extensions would bring.

Trams from Altrincham and Eccles turned at St Peter's Square, standing in the short section between the stop and Princess Street and using the crossover between there and G-Mex. On arrival at G-Mex trams had to wait for a clear road into St Peter's Square before completing their journey. There were no such problems at Victoria as a crossover was already available for trams turning back there.

Metrolink mounted a huge publicity campaign with large posters sited across the city centre and laid on replacement buses to bridge the gap, although these were often elusive and most passengers preferred to walk or use the free Metroshuttle services.

During the summer of 2009 the city centre was completely cut off by the reconstruction work. In the picture at the bottom of the opposite page, with just seven weeks to go, work is progressing at Shudehill interchange. The stop had only been open for three years and the platforms had been built originally at full height throughout their length so needed no further work. Major work was, however, necessary at Piccadilly Gardens where the tracks had to be completely re-aligned to accommodate the much larger island platform needed for the anticipated traffic increase.

On the right a tram stands in the temporary stub end in Mosley Street while waiting to move down to the stop to pick up passengers for Eccles. Below, a sign on the fencing in Mosley Street does seem to state the obvious, although it does direct prospective passengers to St Peter's Square.

MediaCityUK

A short branch off the Eccles line to serve the Lowry Centre in Salford Quays had been included in the original Metrolink 2000 plan, subject to private sector funding, and a strip of land had been reserved and points and a crossover had been put in but clipped out of use. However, the money was not forthcoming and the plan lapsed until the BBC decided to move much of its operations to a site at the adjacent South Quay. This proposal quickly grew into a massive 36-acre development known as MediaCityUK, housing other creative, digital and media businesses, plus the University of Salford as well as a number of high rise apartment blocks, shops, bars and an hotel. The quarter-mile branch became the first section of Phase 3A to open when, on 20th September 2010, the Piccadilly to Eccles service began running in and out of the branch using the triangle of tracks in both directions.

On a sunny October day a Piccadilly to Eccles service takes the west to north chord at Broadway, while below another tram stands in the terminus while the driver changes ends to take it on to Eccles. This was the first station to be built to the higher standard now in evidence.

South Manchester

The 6.1 mile South Manchester line leaves the Altrincham route immediately west of Trafford Bar Station to join the track bed of the long abandoned line from Central to Stockport and eventually London (St Pancras). There are seven intermediate stops *en route*. It travels through a disused bridge under the Altrincham route to provide grade segregation between the two lines. Construction began in 2009, clearing the undergrowth, replacing the drainage, widening the cutting where necessary and building new tram stops. Track-laying started in 2010 and the line opened as far as St Werburgh's Road, Chorlton on 7th July 2011.

Initially the service ran to a temporary terminus at Victoria, but when the first stage of the Rochdale line opened on 13th June 2012 it was extended through to Oldham. Further extensions followed, to Shaw and Crompton on 16th December 2012, to Rochdale Railway Station on 28th February 2013, to East Didsbury on 23rd March 2013 and finally to Rochdale Town Centre on 31st March 2014.

The South Manchester line leaves the Altrincham route immediately beyond the Trafford Bar stop. The points were laid in ready for the construction during a possession in the summer of 2009. In the upper picture, taken a few weeks later, the outward line can just be seen swinging away to the left in the distance beyond the tram, while the inward line passes under the Altrincham tracks by a long-disused bridge before curving sharply upwards to join it just before the platform end.

On the right a tram has gained the track bed of the former Midland route through the Peak District to St Pancras and is heading south to St Werburgh's Road. In the background can be seen the connection to the new Old Trafford Depot just beyond the crossover.

Chorlton tram stop is built on the site of the former Chorlton-cum-Hardy station of the old Cheshire Lines Committee. Access is from Wilbraham Road and directly from a supermarket car park immediately to the right of the picture.

The temporary terminus of the line was at St Werburgh's Road on the site of the former Chorlton Junction where lines to Stockport and Guide Bridge diverged. On the left a tram runs under St Werburgh's Road Bridge. The lift and stairs can be seen on the right.

In the lower view of the stop from the bridge, the footpath on the left follows the line of the former Guide Bridge route. In the distance can be seen Mauldeth Road bridge, just before which the proposed Airport branch will curve away up the hill to the right to join Mauldeth Road itself.

Four pictures of the East Didsbury extension on a sunny June afternoon in 2013. Clockwise from the top, a Rochdale to East Didsbury service runs into the stop at West Didsbury, another East Didsbury-bound tram arrives at Didsbury Village stop and two views of the East Didsbury terminus, which is also a major park and ride site.

Oldham and Rochdale

The 14-mile route to Oldham and Rochdale shares the tracks of the Bury line northwards out of Victoria. At Irk Valley Junction, just after emerging from Collyhurst tunnel, it swings away to the right on a long abandoned viaduct to Smedley Junction where it follows the track bed of the former loop line by which Yorkshire expresses avoided the steeper original route up Miles Platting Bank. At Thorp's Bridge trams cross the main lines by a curved concrete viaduct to join the former Oldham Loop line which closed in 2009 to enable work to start on its conversion to Metrolink.

The route opened as far as a temporary terminus at Oldham Mumps on 13th June 2012, extending to Shaw and Crompton on 16th December and to Rochdale Railway Station on 28th February 2013. The final link to the Town Centre Interchange opened on 31st March 2014. Services from Rochdale run through to East Didsbury on the South Manchester line.

The benefit to the local community of a rapid transit line can be seen from Government figures which show that the average value of property in Oldham has increased by more than 11% during 2013, the biggest rise in the country outside London. Industry experts say that there is a huge demand for houses near to Metrolink stops.

Intended to be the flagship of the network, the futuristic station at Central Park, an upmarket technology park in Newton Heath, was completed in 2005 but, due to the subsequent withdrawal of funding, stood unused for seven years.

Central Park finally came into use when the line opened as far as Oldham in June 2012. In the upper picture a tram is ready to depart.

Just beyond Central Park and visible from the platform end, is the spectacular inverted 'T' pre-stressed concrete viaduct carrying Metrolink services over the main railway line to Yorkshire and on to the former railway alignment of the Oldham loop. The bridge incorporates both vertical and horizontal curves into a single span. A tram bound for St Werburgh's Road drops down from the viaduct and runs into Central Park Station shortly after the opening of the line.

Typical of the new tram stops which have replaced the old railway stations along the route is Hollinwood. The former station has been demolished and replaced by a modern structure with staircases and a lift. Situated just off the M60 motorway, Hollinwood also has a new park and ride facility.

The Oldham Town Centre line opened on 27January 2014, serving four new stops at Westwood, King Street, Oldham Central and the new Mumps Interchange. An East Didsbury-bound tram is pictured arriving at Oldham Central in early March.

At Derker the former station has again been completely replaced and a large car park built with access directly on to the inward platform As the main park and ride facility for the north side of Oldham, Derker is one of the most heavily used stops on the line.

The old BR station at Shaw and Crompton was situated on the north side of Beal Lane level crossing. To alleviate delays to traffic caused by the greatly increased number of journeys, the new tram stop was located on the south side. To accommodate the additional journeys which will turn back at Shaw when the final planned frequency is introduced, a bay platform was built, which makes it at this time the only stop with more than two platforms.

Metrolink reached Shaw and Crompton on 16th December 2012, the trams using the bay platform. Unlike the rest of the system, there are some quite lengthy rural stretches beyond Derker. In the mid-summer sunshine a Rochdale-bound service approaches Jubilee Pit level crossing.

On the right, Milnrow is another example of a former BR station being completely replaced by a tram stop.

The upper photograph, taken from the platform of Rochdale Railway Station, shows its proximity to the Metrolink stop, where an East Didsbury-bound tram is about to leave. The imposing building in the background is the church of St John the Evangelist.

From the station the Metrolink line runs partly on segregated track and partly on street to the terminus of the route in the town centre transport interchange. In the picture below unit 3005 has just arrived from East Didsbury and the driver has not yet changed ends and reset the destination display. On the right is the new bus station and in the background the new Rochdale Council offices.

East Manchester

The six-mile East Manchester line runs from Piccadilly to Ashton-under-Lyne on a mixture of segregated alignment and on-street running, following a completely new route through the regeneration areas of Ancoats and Beswick and serving the Eastlands-Sports City complex as far as Clayton Hall. From here it continues on-street along Ashton New Road through Droylsden to Audenshaw, where it once again follows a segregated route along Lord Sheldon Way to Ashton-under-Lyne, terminating at the town's Transport Interchange.

Construction began in the summer of 2009, demolishing property in Ancoats and along Ashton New Road. Major building work included the Great Ancoats Street and Alan Turing Way underpasses and bridging the River Medlock at Holt Town. Track laying and tram stop construction continued during 2010 and 2011 and the line opened as far as Droylsden on 11th February 2013, the service running through from Bury.

In March 2010 the Department approved a further extension to Ashton-under-Lyne; work starting soon after and the line opening on 9th October 2013.

The East Manchester line utilises the former head shunt at Piccadilly and leaves the tram station by a re-opened entrance to the undercroft. It immediately crosses Sheffield Street where a tram is seen below on its way to Droylsden.

After crossing Sheffield Street the track follows the line of Chapeltown Street, where a new turnback siding has been provided between the running lines for services from Eccles, Media City and Altrincham. An Altrincham-bound tram leaves the siding to take up service at Piccadilly.

The line then runs straight up Chapeltown Street and dives under Great Ancoats Street by an underpass. On the left a Droylsden-bound tram emerges from the underpass with one of the spectacular high rise buildings of the New Islington development in the background. In the lower picture an Altrincham to Droylsden service arrives at the New Islington stop with two new apartment blocks in the background.

After a short stretch of street running along Merrill Street, shared with general traffic, the line crosses the new bridge over the River Medlock and runs into Holt Town stop. A Bury service is seen approaching the stop. It is hard to believe that this almost rural scene was until recently an area of run down or derelict industrial units, but is now a linear park following the Medlock Valley to Eastlands. The centrepiece of the Eastlands sports complex is the Etihad Stadium, built for 2002 Commonwealth Games and now the home of Manchester City Football Club. Extra services are run on match days to cater for the crowds. After leaving Etihad Campus stop, the line swings underneath Alan Turing Way and then turns round the corner parallel to Ashton New Road and the Velopark stop serving the Asda superstore and the Velodrome.

Just after Clayton Hall the East Manchester line runs on street as far as Audenshaw. In the picture above a Bury to Droylsden unit crosses Clayton Lane and runs into Clayton Hall stop. The church of St Cross forms the backdrop across Ashton New Road.

The next stop is at Edge Lane, squeezed between Manor Road and Manchester Road where a Droylsden to Bury service is about to depart.

The original terminus was at Droylsden, where again the stop is situated in the middle of the road. The route was extended from here to Ashton-under-Lyne transport interchange on 9th October 2013.

On its approach to Ashton-under-Lyne town centre Metrolink runs on a segregated right of way alongside, or in the centre of Lord Sheldon Way. At Ashton Moss there is a 200 vehicle park and ride facility providing easy access to both Ashton and Manchester. In the upper picture a double unit runs into the stop on an Ashton to Bury working. In the centre view another Bury-bound tram heads for Ashton West stop with the IKEA superstore in the background.

The terminus at Ashton is located next to the town centre bus station and is a short walk from the railway station. On an extremely wet Sunday morning in November 2013, a tram stands in the platform ready to start its long journey across Manchester to Bury.

Still to come

In the spring of 2014 work is progressing on the Airport line with major infrastructure complete and track laid on most of the route. The target for completion is 2015.

At the end of October 2013 formal agreement was reached for the construction of the second city crossing (2CC) which will see trams run from Victoria Station along Corporation Street, Cross Street and Princess Street to rejoin the existing network at St Peter's Square, where a new four-platform stop will be built.

The first section of the route between Victoria and Exchange Square is currently under construction and is scheduled to open by 2015, allowing a Shaw to Exchange Square service to be operated. The full route is expected to open in 2017.

Associated with this is the current rebuilding of Victoria Station which includes doubling the capacity of the Metrolink stop by providing a further two platform faces. While the work progresses trams are passing through the station without stopping.

The long awaited Trafford Park spur from the existing but so far unused junction at Pomona received financial approval from the Government during 2013 and will include a park and ride facility at the Trafford Centre. The remainder of the line from there to Port Salford is still under consideration. The new route would require another 10 trams taking the fleet up to 104.

Finally, the car parks at Radcliffe and Whitefield on the Bury line are being extended by adding an upper deck, which will provide an additional 203 parking spaces on the route.

A double unit passes through the Victoria working site on a Bury to Altrincham service.